nat Hist
1358

WILDLIFE ENCOUNTERS

WILDLIFE ENCOUNTERS

Photographs by Bob & Ira Spring
Text by Ira Spring
Edited by Harvey Manning

*Buffalo in snowstorm near Old Faithful Lodge. A few moments
later he chased me up a tree.*

Bighorn sheep in Glacier National Park

Library of Congress Cataloging in Publication Data

Spring, Robert, 1918-
   Wildlife encounters.

   Includes index.
   1. Zoology—Northwest, Pacific.   2. Animals,
Legends and stories of.   3. Spring, Robert,
1918-   I. Spring, Ira.   II. Title.
QL212.S67   596'.09'795   75-23133
ISBN 0-87564-012-5

FIRST EDITION

CONTENTS

Elk wading Firehole River, Yellowstone National Park

Rain-drenched yellow violet on Rugged Ridge, Olympic National Park

PREFACE

I've spent most of my life roaming wildlands of the Northwest, first in my youth for recreation and then as a professional photographer. The mountains were my first love, as they were for my twin brother, Bob. We came to the life of the out-of-doors by family inheritance. On their honeymoon our parents paddled a canoe up Puget Sound to its head, where a farmer portaged them to Hood Canal for more days of paddling, nights of beach-camping. As newlyweds they lived on the Sound and Dad walked the beach 3 miles to and from work in Olympia.

In the final weeks of World War I Dad's brother was killed in battle and the folks moved east to be near our grandparents. It was there, in Jamestown, New York, Bob and I were born in 1918.

My memories of the East are skimpy: winter tramps in the woods, skis with toe straps for bindings, canoe trips to remote lakes a hundred miles north of Toronto. Undoubtedly the lakes were teeming with wildlife but, being just 5 years old, the only thing I remember about those trips is skinny-dipping before breakfast.

By the time Bob and I were 7 our folks had enough of the East and returned to Puget Sound, settling in Shelton. The Olympic Mountains were close and the first summer Dad took Bob and me for a climb of Mt. Elinor. The trail was poorly marked and we ended up on Mt. Rose.

Family vacations were devoted to canoe trips around the Sound, camping on beaches wherever we felt like it. In later years, watching the subdivisions sprawl, I realized somebody owned all that saltwater property. In those days, though, the shores were empty and wild, houses few and far between. Springs and creeks provided plenty of pure drinking water and there was lots of driftwood for fires.

At the age of 12 Bob and I joined the Boy Scouts. We were fortunate to have a scoutmaster —Tom Martin, a politician by trade—who loved the mountains. Our Scout camp was at Lena Lake, even now a 2-mile hike from the road. Every summer we spent 3 weeks at camp exploring the high Olympics. Tom introduced us to true mountaineering—leaving trails and striking off cross-country through alpine meadows and rockslides and snowfields, learning to navigate basins and ridges in the dense fogs which engulfed us days at a time.

Deeply as Bob and I enjoyed the mountains for themselves, I wonder if our interest in the flora and fauna wasn't spurred by the neckerchief emblem a Scout was awarded for being first to see a new animal or flower. On a Scout hike I saw my first elk. I don't recall whose neckerchief got the emblem but after 40 years I feel a thrill at the memory of the herd galloping down the side of Mt. Stone. It looked and sounded like a cattle stampede in a Wild West movie.

In 1930, to celebrate the company's 50th anniversary, Eastman Kodak gave every 12-year-old in the United States a box Brownie. Right away Bob and I found mountains and cameras go together. With those little Brownies we began what eventually became our careers.

When we graduated from high school we looked for a college offering a course in photography. In contrast to today, there was only one in our area, Ellensburg Normal (now Central Washington State College), and that because of a single professor. Glenn Hogue thought photography was an art, not just the science of chemical reactions and bending light rays. He drove us to take picture after picture, never stopping. It was only a 3-hour course but we frequently were in the studio and darkroom until midnight. We couldn't have had a more dedicated and inspiring teacher.

In college years I was lucky enough to get a summer job as night janitor at Paradise Inn on Mt. Rainier. During the day, when I was supposed to be sleeping, I lay on a heather-covered knoll watching shadows move across the mountain and figuring camera angles. Sometimes I spotted little white specks in the green meadows of Van Trump Park, a mile away beyond the Nisqually Glacier. Mountain goats!

After World War II Bob and I decided to try to make a living as outdoor photographers. We specialized in glaciers, intrigued by the towering cliffs of icefalls, the beautiful blues in deep crevasses, the incredible sculptures of seracs. New York editors were fascinated too and our work was published in every well-known magazine of the 1940s and 50s. Our greatest helper, though, was Chester Gibbon, Sunday Feature Editor of the Seattle *Times*. Before his death he used several hundred of our picture stories.

Al Salisbury of Seattle's Superior Publishing Company was another whose faith in our work was invaluable. In 1950, when we were just getting started, he published our first book, *High Adventure*, which opened to us the doors of many New York advertising agencies and publishers.

While the book was in press I showed press sheets to the editor of *U.S. Camera*. He warned me to make sure the publisher had the reproductions done by a good engraver. I pointed out the prints he was looking at *were* reproductions!

Bob married Norma before the war. Though previously an indoor person, a music teacher, she took to the trails as if born to the life. Eventually Bob shifted to travel photography, visiting famous tourist areas all over the world, yet always keeping an eye out for wildlife. He's gotten exciting pictures of animals in Alaska. He's also missed some good ones. Once he was photographing a line of fishermen on the banks of a river when an enormous grizzly bear came by for his share of the salmon. As the brute lumbered down the beach the fishermen scattered. Not having a telephoto lens handy, Bob scattered too. Without a picture.

In 1947, while photographing a climbing class of The Mountaineers for a Seattle *Times* story, I naturally focused on the best-looking (actually, the only) girl in the crowd. One thing led to another and in 1949 Pat and I were married. She came of a family of ardent fishermen, was already an enthusiastic hiker, and therefore saw nothing strange in spending the first week of our honeymoon hiking in the Olympics, the second and third weeks photographing a Mountaineer outing around Glacier Peak. John was born in 1950 and Vicky in 1953. Both were backpacking (on our backs) by the age of 4 months. They grew up knowing if they weren't good kids they'd be left home. Mostly they were good kids.

In our early married years we hiked and climbed and skied in the Olympics, Cascades, and Canadian Rockies, occasionally the Tetons and Colorado Rockies, taking pictures used in calendars, advertisements, and more books. Then we expanded our horizons.

In 1959, when John and Vicky were in the first and third grades, we rented a chalet for a year near Chamonix in the French Alps. The scenery was tremendous and so was the hiking—we thoroughly enjoyed taking the kids up Alps in cable cars and walking long trails back down to our chalet. Something was lacking, though—wildlife. The only animals we saw (cows don't count) were a half-dozen chamois in a small preserve along the Aletsch Galcier in Switzerland.

In 1963 we rented a small house on the side of Mt. Fuji. Much of the year the four of us huddled around a kerosene stove in an unsuccessful attempt to keep warm. But we saw Fuji almost every day. Again we missed the wildlife, which

except in remote parts of Japan has been exterminated. Some temple grounds are roamed by deer—free but not very wild. Every species of bird is considered potential meat on the table. One hunter proudly showed us his bag of a half-dozen wren-sized birds.

Our next journey abroad was to Scandinavia, where we spent 6 months of 1967, including a full summer photographing a children's book about a boy who lived on Norway's Geiranger Fiord. The boy was an avid hiker and skier and led us to glorious views of the peaks that rise straight up from saltwater to snowcapped summits that seem much higher than they really are. The only wild animals we saw were reindeer. As I can testify after a scary sleigh ride over the steppes of northern Lapland, chasing a running herd, the reindeer is technically domesticated but definitely not tame.

We have innumerable fond memories of our foreign travels. Yet with the maturity of age I've come to realize there is, in truth, no place like home. The Olympics aren't as spectacular as other ranges I've seen but that's where I grew up and I'm happiest of all roaming the wildlands there.

Also with maturity I've grown to understand how much I owe the men and women who labored to establish the national parks and wilderness areas in which I've spent most of my life. Because these dedicated people had succeeded so well in their efforts, for years I never publicly protested the steady advance of logging, river-damming, and highway-building into unprotected wildlands. There seemed an infinite supply of trails remaining.

But at some point along the way "progress" took just one too many of my old trails and I got mad. I saw that though there might be sufficient wildlands for my own needs, if my children were to have hiking room I was going to have to add my voice to the chorus of "wild-eyed conservationists."

As a young hiker I seldom saw anyone else on the trail. Now there are 200,000 backpackers in the Puget Sound area and 6,000,000 in the United States—but over half the trails that existed in Washington State when I began hiking have been destroyed. We can't afford to lose any more—but we are, every year. That's why as time has passed my books and picture stories increasingly have stressed the need to preserve wilderness.

From remarks in this book a reader may suppose I'm flatly opposed to hunting. I'm not. Certainly in my travels I've seen the sport at its

Bighorn lambs on side of Mt. Everts in Yellowstone National Park

Deer near Mammoth Hot Springs

worst: hunters' camps piled high with empty beer and whisky bottles, commercial packers and their 30-horse strings hauling gunners into the wilderness and turning the back country into a battlefield. However, I've met hunters who enjoy the wilderness as much as I and have a far better knowledge of the wildlife. Pat's father is an example. If he'd been raised with a camera in his hands instead of a gun he'd have a magnificent collection of pictures, but he grew up on Vancouver Island surrounded by wildlife throughout his youth and his family depended on his hunting for food.

Nevertheless, though I acknowledge hunting as a sport as legitimate as hiking or photography, I feel the non-hunter is short-changed. The wildlife "belongs" to everyone. The majority of us enjoy seeing "our share" alive. But the minority which wants "its share" dead acts as if it owned *all* the animals.

A California study reported in the January 1974 issue of *Western Wildlands* showed that 80 percent of the recreational "use" of wildlife is by non-hunters, people who simply look and maybe photograph. But the 20 percent who hunt so reduce the wildlife populations and terrorize and scatter the remnants that the 80 percent rarely see animals—except in such large national parks as Yellowstone and Olympic where creatures of the interior never come under fire.

Granted, some animal populations, notably deer, quickly expand beyond the feeding capacity of their ranges and must be controlled. However, though hunting keeps down the numbers of a species, it does not *preserve* the species. Hunters shoot the best animals, the ones most fit to perpetuate their kind. The European stag of today is smaller than that hunted by kings a century ago. Similarly, selective killing is endangering the quality—and in the long run, the ability to survive—of the bighorn sheep.

For the sake of preserving wildlife, and for the sake of the 80 percent of us who enjoy animals and birds alive rather than dead, every western state should have at least one *huge* game sanctuary large enough to protect the animals in all seasons, the population controlled naturally by predators, assisted when necessary by rangers who weed out the sick and scrawny (just as do the predators) rather than the big and healthy. Moreover, certain species such as the mountain goat and bighorn sheep should be protected absolutely from hunting, in or out of a sanctuary. There are too few for looking, none to spare for shooting.

Unfortunately, wildlife "protection" is governed by the dollar—the lobbying of the gun industry, the state game departments financed by hunting licenses. For its own economic interests the photography industry ought to, but doesn't, lobby in opposition to the gun industry—more money is spent photographing animals than killing them. The government should start selling non-hunting licenses and use the fees to support sanctuaries.

Some of my best friends are hunters. Some of my best friends' best friends are dogs, and that's another problem for wildlife. Of course, no single dog is going to chase away all the animals and birds, but the cumulative effect of hundreds of dogs in a wilderness definitely upsets the natural balance. Certainly, wherever there are lots of dogs, a hiker sees less wildlife. Unfortunately, despite warning signs, even national park trails are being overwhelmed, dog owners feeling it's worth risking a small fine so their pals can also enjoy the park. Funny, many of these dog-owners are staunch defenders of wilderness. However, if they don't become convinced dogs are not a proper part of wilderness, eventually the only animals any of us will see in the back country are dogs.

If maturity has made me angry about the loss of trail country and the unfair sharing of wildlife, and too many dogs where they don't belong, it's had other effects as well. For one, I find the trails a bit steeper and the pack a lot heavier. I've slowed down a little—enough so I no longer push on in haste to see the view around the next bend, no longer am impatient to climb out of the green world onto glaciers and crags. Now that I'm not always running, I have time to see the beauty at my feet. I admire glaciers as much as ever, but I find flowers equally fascinating. I enjoy gaining a peak-top panorama as much as ever, but spend more time stalking animals in their mountain homes.

Actually, "stalking" is the wrong word. "Stumbling on animals" is more honest. Often I've rounded a corner and met a deer, bear, elk, goat, marten, or ermine. Usually the encounters are as surprising to me as the animal and are too fleeting for a camera to be unlimbered. Other times it's too early in the morning or too late in the evening and the light is wrong. But occasionally luck is with me, the telephoto lens is on the camera when I need it, the light is just right, and I bring away from the meeting something besides a story and a memory. They haven't all gotten away. From the lucky accidents have come the photographs in this book.

PHOTOGRAPHY

Life was simple for Bob and me when the only photographic gear we owned was the box Brownies given us by Eastman Kodak. However, though we got a few good pictures with them, in a few years we graduated to more sophisticated equipment.

At the time we decided to try our luck as professionals, nearly all publishers insisted on 4×5-inch or larger film. We chose the Speed Graphic, rugged and compact enough to carry in a pack but opening to a full-sized view camera. With a supply of film it weighs about 20 pounds, a cruel addition to a hiking or climbing pack that already is 30 pounds or more, but the results compensate for the pain. The Speed Graphic is virtually worthless for animal photography, of course, since unpacking and setting up take 5 minutes or so. Animals aren't often that patient.

In the 1960s printers learned to obtain good reproduction from 35mm film, which thus became standard for the majority of professionals. The smaller camera was a blessing for Bob when his interest shifted to travel; flying around with the Speed Graphic would have cost him a fortune in overweight charges. I still love the quality of the large negatives. However, as flowers began occupying more of my attention, I added a 35mm to my pack for close-ups. Then came a 200mm lens for animals and finally a 1000mm lens for birds.

The perfecting of 35mm reproduction has done nothing to lighten my pack as I generally can't bring myself to leave the Speed Graphic behind. I need only one set of lenses but carry three 35mm camera bodies loaded with different films: a low-speed Kodachrome for best color and sharpness; High Speed Ektachrome for dark or windy days, which in the areas I travel seems to be *most* days; Tri-X for black and white.

All this is more of a load than ought to be saddled on a single aching back. My son, John, is no help anymore; he's a fine photographer but has his own projects. Wife Pat and daughter Vicky are my patient mules—and my very capable partners. While I'm using the Speed Graphic or a 35mm, they're busy with the others. We switch cameras so much and take so many exposures of the same subject it's nearly impossible to remember who took what. My guess is that in this book the color picture of the swans is Vicky's, the color pictures of the elk in snow, pika, marmots, bear cubs, and undoubtedly more, are Pat's. Bob and I are the only ones who bother with black-and-white shots so I know we took those.

The mechanics of the modern camera are fairly easy to master. Any hiker who takes a lot of pictures is bound to get at least a few exceptional ones. Young people often show me portfolios of photos I'd be proud to call my own and ask advice on how to break in as a professional. I tell them that before they can seriously make the rounds of publishers (newspaper, magazines, books) on a regular basis, with the hope of earning a living, they must have not a few exceptional pictures but thousands. You may visit an editor with a hundred superb photos (your opinion) and he'll flip through the stack and—and if you're lucky—find one or two he likes.

I warn that the life of an outdoor photographer is not all fun and games. Yes, you spend much of the year in the wilderness, and that's wonderful. But for every hour on the trail you spend 2 hours in the darkroom—and then more hours selling, paying many many visits to editors, writing countless letters.

By definition, it's the selling (not the artistry, which we all strive for) that distinguishes a professional from an amateur. Planning is the crux. You have to go places potentially offering plentiful opportunities for good pictures, and you have to arrange your schedule to be there in the right season and at the right time of day. And you have to arrange for the right weather! You constantly have to keep in mind the needs of editors and their tastes, which may not be your own. But planning isn't everything. You also have to have a huge amount of luck.

My professional friends and I agree that for pure fun the amateur has the best of it, taking pictures purely for his own esthetic pleasure and that of his friends. However, I never try to discourage anyone from seeking to make a career of outdoor photography. For myself I can't imagine any other life.

Overleaf: South side of Mt. Baker from Park Butte in the North Cascades, Washington, goat and marmot country

RACCOON

A raccoon family used to live under the front porch of Mt. Rainier National Park's Longmire Inn. Tourists fed them by hand and occasionally got a finger nipped. The raccoons became beggars and beggars aren't very natural, which a national park is supposed to be, so rangers sealed the holes under the porch and the raccoons moved on.

Evidently they moved to Longmire Campground. One November evening when our son John wasn't yet 4 years old we were setting up camp. Suddenly a raccoon ran out of the darkness and flipped our food box over and scampered off with the bag of trail candy. Heaven forbid! Anything but that! Johnny went screaming in pursuit. I grabbed a flashlight and followed. The coon scrambled up a tall tree and ate the whole bag of goodies. All that drifted down were bits of paper and a rubberband.

Next morning, after we awoke in our tent, my wife Pat furiously accused me of hiding an important item of her lingerie. I pled not guilty but she wasn't convinced and kept muttering about my so-called sense of humor. We searched the tent. No luck. Finally she dressed without it and we crawled outside. And there was an entire wardrobe of clothing scattered around for everyone in the campground to see. Including her missing bra. I guess young women don't worry as much now as they did then about public display of unmentionables. But it was the raccoon's practical joke, not mine. He'd sure been quiet that night, when he invaded our tent.

Pat had a reason to suspect me. On the second week of our honeymoon we had an assignment to photograph a Mountaineer outing at Glacier Peak. One night a heck of a storm blew in and broke the guyline of our mountain tent. I fumbled around in the tent and found some new line, went out in the rain and wind and tied us up again. In the morning Pat couldn't find her bra. Even if it is small, you just can't lose something like that in a tent, but she did. Once outside she saw it, tangled in the guyline, flapping like a flag. She still doesn't think it got there by accident.

At Longmire in those days it would've been easy to take all kinds of raccoon pictures but I always was in a hurry to climb up on the mountain.

It was in Redwood National Park, while stalking blue heron on tideflats at the mouth of the Klamath River, I got my next good chance. The herons spooked whenever I came within a quarter-mile of them so I wasn't having any luck. However, I spotted a coon hunting in a small tributary. Once in a while he gave me a glance but mostly he was busy turning over rocks in the stream looking for something to eat—what, I couldn't tell, though he was only 20 feet off. Several times a "something" got away and he made a leap for it and missed. I'd have enjoyed watching him longer but the tide was coming in and I had to retreat.

Night raider in Longmire Campground, Mt. Rainier National Park

Raccoon feeding on tide flats at mouth of Klamath River, Redwood National Park

ELK

I first encountered the Olympic elk on a Boy Scout hike from Lower Lena Lake. We'd climbed a sketchy path to Upper Lena Lake and then followed game trails through meadows of Baldy Ridge to a camp at Lake of the Angels, a little tarn on the side of Mt. Stone. Next day our noses discovered what our leader called an "elk barn," an area protected from wind by alpine trees, heavily tramped and stinking like a barn. A half-mile farther we rounded a ridge and stampeded a herd of 80 or more elk. The last we saw they were plunging downhill into timber of the Hamma Hamma valley. I snapped some shots with my box Brownie but they weren't worth saving.

In 1946 my brother Bob, his wife Norma, and I were doing a photo story for the Seattle *Times* on the High Divide, across the Hoh valley from Mt. Olympus. Early in the morning, a short distance above Hoh Lake, we spotted elk grazing in a meadow. Bob hid in a grove of trees above them while I ducked down a ravine and climbed a timbercone below. Just as I was getting into good position I stumbled over a cow sleeping a hundred feet from the others. She lept up in fright and stampeded the herd. Unfortunately they didn't run up towards Bob but down towards me and I was so close my camera caught nothing but a cloud of dust. That's been my luck. To this day I've not taken an elk picture in the Olympics that pleases me.

One of the few times I've gone out specifically to photograph animals was in the fall of 1973, when I was determined to at last get one good elk

Elk on High Divide, Olympic National Park

shot for a book on Olympic National Park. My wife Pat and I climbed the trail from Soleduck River, first in rain, then in clouds, and groped our way along the High Divide to a camp at Hoh Lake. We saw elk tracks on the trail but no elk.

The morning was clear and we dashed up Bogachiel Peak for the panoramic view from glaciers to ocean. In the typical Olympic habit, clouds soon formed at our feet and before we could locate the elk herd fog again engulfed us. We asked every hiker on the trail if they'd seen elk and finally one said he sure had—he'd counted 102 in a meadow at the head of Canyon Creek. The fog blew away and Pat and I hastily broke camp and hiked to Canyon Creek. The elk were there, all right, but had moved into the woods. One fuzzy shot of 20 cows in a small glade was my total reward.

Pat had brought a plastic elk call. I scoffed. It sounded like no elk I'd ever heard. After listening to a couple of bulls bugling at each other in the forest, she imitated them and to my surprise they bellowed back. In fact, she got into quite an interesting conversation.

We went out stalking. At first we were quiet as possible, but when cracking dry branches and starting a rock slide didn't set off a stampede, we realized elk make so much of that kind of noise themselves they'd be frightened only by such unfamiliar sounds as our voices. We pitched our tent in a strategic spot and hid inside to wait for elk. All night we heard them crashing around in the woods, making a worse racket than a Boy Scout troop.

In the wee hours, light enough to see but too dark for pictures, Pat again blew on her elk call. The response was instantaneous and after a brisk exchange a magnificent bull appeared. He bugled, stamped his hooves, and tore up a shrub with his antlers—obviously challenging Pat to come out and fight. She was too chicken so the elk stomped away. No pictures.

I haven't done any better in Mt. Rainier National Park. Several years ago my daughter Vicky and I were having lunch beside Shriner Lake when we saw a cow elk approaching the far side of the lake. We kept very still but she spotted us. Apparently unable to figure out what we were, she kept walking toward the lake, her head turned in our direction. The silly beast was so busy watching us she stumbled over a bank and fell in the lake. One big splash and an undignified retreat. On that trip I was working on a trail guidebook and therefore didn't have a telephoto

Elk calves in the South Wyoming Range, a proposed wilderness

with me. Again, no pictures. Just a funny memory.

The problem with trying to photograph elk in Olympic and Mt. Rainier National Parks is that spacious as these parks are, heavy winter snows force elk outside the boundaries, where the gunners wait, making the animals extremely wary even in summer. We often see them but seldom long enough for a picture. Only in Yellowstone National Park, so vast the elk can spend their whole lives in the interior, never being shot at, are they really wild and fearless. In summer they scatter and travelers may see no more than one or two at a time but in winter they graze by the hundreds in the Lamar Valley, along the all-year Cooke City-Mammoth Hot Springs road.

I had a narrow escape one winter in Yellowstone. I'd singled out a nice-looking bull from a group feeding beside the Fire Hole River. I edged as near as he'd allow and jockeyed around to get a steam vent in the background. While intent on my target bull, suddenly I heard a grating noise behind me, looked over my shoulder—and about 10 feet away stood a second and very irritated bull, glowering and grinding his teeth. I was in "his territory" and in no uncertain terms he was telling me to beat it—which I promptly did.

Much pleasanter was an encounter on a 10,000-foot ridge in the South Wyoming Range Wilderness Study Area. Vicky and I surprised a herd of maybe 40 elk. The cows and bulls ran off but four small calves didn't get the message. I talked to them and sang a lullaby, slowly moving closer. They were brimming with curiosity, torn between running away or listening to my songs. I got within 50 feet before they decided my voice wasn't all that great.

Elk in large numbers once roamed the Northwest from the Rocky Mountains to the ocean. In most places they long ago were hunted to extermination or starved out by cattle overgrazing their ranges. In some areas where they've been replanted, as in the Sawtooth Mountains of Idaho, and hunting is controlled, a few elk eke out an existence. They can't compete with cattle, though, and never will make enough of a comeback to be easily visible to the tourist.

The surviving Northwest herds summer in the high country and winter in the lowlands—to the consternation of farmers. To save the herds (for the hunters) while keeping the farmers quiet, state game departments feed elk in winter—so they won't invade the farms which have invaded their winter ranges. The best luck I've had photographing elk was at the Oak Creek feeding lot, near Yakima in Central Washington. Once we parked our camper on a snowcovered road there. No elk were around when we went to bed but during the night the moon rose and we awoke to find ourselves surrounded by over 100 animals. In heavy snowfalls hunger so numbs their fear of man all but the wariest bulls come to the feeding lots, where they chomp hay a few feet from hundreds of camera-clicking visitors—including me.

The feeding saves Yakima Valley apple orchards from nibbling and elk from starvation but it's no substitute for Yellowstone-size sanctuaries. Accustomed to handouts, elk show up at the lots whether or not snow is on the ground. They become semi-domesticated, easy targets for the fall slaughter. Many hunters I know who love to stalk deer draw the line at going for elk. They say it's about as much sport as shooting dairy cows.

A herd of elk feeding along the Firehole River, Yellowstone National Park

Elk in Washington State Game Department's Oak Creek Feeding Station on the east side of the Cascades

Beaver in the backwater of Bow River, Banff National Park

BEAVER

A dam builder with no regard for what he floods. A logger who cuts and runs with no thought of sustained yield, who often overcuts and has to abandon his home. He doesn't even file an environmental impact statement.

All in all he sounds worse than a combination of the Army Engineers and the timber industry, and he would be too if he could drive a bulldozer. Fortunately, his work is done solely by teeth, paws, and tail. Actually, the Army Engineers and the timber industry might be environmentally sound if confined to using the same tools.

Beaver are basically nocturnal and wary. In my whole life I've seen only two and the solitary picture in our file was taken by Bob at Banff. I have, however, seen a lot of their workings. And also heard some. One quiet night at Fish Lake in the Alpine Lakes area of the Cascades the silence was shattered by a "CRACK!" as a beaver slapped his tail on the water a few feet from our tent. Why he did it, I don't know.

I was canoeing with a park ranger at the mouth of the Klamath River in California when we surprised an adult beaver and a youngster on the riverbank. They lept in the water and the adult swam under the canoe and was gone. The youngster got confused and swam in circles, stirring up such a cloud of mud we finally couldn't see him.

Al Salisbury, our publisher, tells of the time he was fishing on the Willamette River in Oregon and spotted a beaver towing a branch of scotchbroom. On seeing him the beaver dove, leaving the branch, or so it seemed. A few minutes later, however, Al saw the scotchbroom moving away, apparently under its own power.

DEER

Deer are the most often and easily seen of large wild animals. Anyone with a camera should have stacks of photographs. I guess the reason I don't is they're as common in the back country as dogs and cats in cities, and have a lot less individuality, so I pass up countless opportunities waiting for the perfect picture.

This doesn't mean I don't enjoy watching them. I've many memories of sitting in alpine meadows gazing at the scenery, hearing a thumpity-thump and a dozen feet away seeing a buck or doe that stops to stare at me, then thumpity-thumps off. And of glancing up from a campfire and finding deer browsing all around in the moonlight, now and then pausing to give us a once-over. I don't mind their curiosity. I'm just as curious about them.

Early one morning, climbing to Gordon Pass on the edge of the Bob Marshall Wilderness in Montana, my daughter Vicky and I came to a 500-foot section of the trail traversing a narrow ledge of sedimentary rock. The ledge might have been laid out by an engineer but doubtless was used by animals eons before man began building trails. We were a hundred feet along the ledge when two bucks started down the other end. Seeing us, one bolted up the trail. The other stood his ground a moment before retreating. We waited to see what would happen. Sure enough, in a couple of minutes a buck poked his head around the corner, peeked at us, and went back. A few more minutes and again he took a peek—obvi- ously getting impatient for his turn at the ledge. We took the hint and hiked on.

Deer have an unreasonable trust in man. Either that or very short memories. A few weeks after the hunting season they lose their fear—even those so badly wounded by bullets they can't possibly live out the winter. I've seen them grazing beside freeways that scare the heck out of me. One summer four deer adopted my father-in-law's garden as their favorite restaurant. He put up a 10-foot chicken-wire fence but they found a gap. One day he surprised a buck in the garden and it jumped through the chicken wire like it was tissue paper. You can still see the big round hole in the fence about 6 feet off the ground.

Their lack of fear isn't all stupidity. As that buck proved, they're great jumpers and strong. Also they're so fast they can outrun just about anything in the wilds except a bullet. And—with the help of camouflage—they're masters at playing hide-and-go-seek. My frequent book collaborator, Harvey Manning, tells of the fall day he was sitting on a moraine in Boston Basin, soaking up scenery. This was before the creation of the North Cascades National Park and suddenly the mountain peace was destroyed by a volley of gunfire in the forest below. A magnificent buck came leaping out of the woods into the meadows, pursued by two hunters blasting away on the run. The buck abruptly stopped—and before Harvey's very eyes vanished as if by magic. The hunters spent hours going back and forth through the autumn-tawny meadows, probably often within a few feet of the buck, and at last gave up and went home.

Deer in the South Wyoming Range

Overleaf: A fawn hiding in the Shark Rock proposed wilderness area of Washington's Gifford Pinchot National Forest

MOUNTAIN GOAT

During my three decades as a professional photographer of wilderness scenes, I've come to think of mountain goats as the living symbol of the high country. They once were frequently seen by hikers in the Cascade Mountains of Washington. Then, in 1948, goat hunting resumed. Now a person is lucky to spot a goat on a distant cliff; the rare closer view usually is a fleeting glimpse as the animal runs in terror.

Far different is the situation in Olympic and Glacier National Parks where, unmolested by hunters, goats gladly share their mountain meadows with humankind, often showing as much curiosity about people as people show about them. It is not too uncommon for a goat to walk up to a resting hiker and look him over, or nibble grass next to a backpacker's tent even though the grass is lusher a few feet away. Tolerant as these gun-free goats are of hikers, they avoid populated areas and roads and thus are seldom seen by motorists.

There's no more thrilling sight than a mountain goat ambling casually up and down a cliff that would scare the wits out of a hiker and make even an experienced climber insist on a rope. The goat—actually an antelope and a distant cousin of the chamois of the Alps—is well-adapted to rugged terrain and harsh climates. In an avalanche fan along the Carbon River I once found a dead goat and had a chance to examine the cup-shaped, rock-gripping soles of its sharp hooves and the thick wool that gives protection from winter storms.

Of course, as that incident proves, the animal makes mistakes, even as do human climbers. And just like human climbers, it must learn mountaincraft. One day while lunching on the Kautz Glacier high on the side of Mt. Rainier I spent an hour watching a family of three holding a climbing school on a nunatak a half-mile distant. An adult would lead the kid up a small rock wall, leap from ledge to ledge, and descend. Then the kid would follow the second adult on another maneuver. I had to chuckle, it was so much like two experienced human mountaineers instructing a beginner.

Several years ago my wife Pat and I hiked up Mt. Angeles in Olympic National Park to "shoot"

Mountain goats on side of Mt. Angeles, Olympic National Park

goats. We came upon a dozen nannies, each with a kid, and for 3 hours edged slowly closer, talking to them and even singing a few songs, and finally got within 30 feet. I was focusing on a nanny and kid when a billy appeared in my ground glass. I tried to bring him in focus but he was moving too fast—toward me! I looked up and he was only 10 feet away and still coming. There was no point trying to explain I wasn't planning indecent liberties with his family. I retreated. He stared me in the eye a minute and then turned and left, followed by nanny and kid.

We stayed on the mountain for a sunset picture and descended in dusk. The trail switchbacked three times through a band of 30 goats grazing in a large meadow. They were so nonchalant they'd barely move out of the way. One large billy stubbornly refused to give ground and we had to make a detour.

Later that summer Vicky, our daughter, joined us for a climb of Mt. Olympus. We camped 3 days on the brink of the Blue Glacier awaiting a break in the weather and during that spell were frequently visited by a lone billy. We never were sure

of his intentions. He didn't seem belligerent but his horns were mighty sharp. One night he grazed around our tent, stumbling over the tentlines. At last he nibbled off the willow branch I'd tied the ridgeline to. A loud PING! and the tent sagged and the goat dashed off. I retied the line and he soon returned. Looking out from my sleeping bag I saw him at the tent door, looking in.

I'm not familiar with what happened to mountain goats in other Western states, but before the arrival of the white man they were very common in the Washington Cascades. In his book, *Steamboats on Lake Chelan*, Bob Byrd tells that in the 1890s thousands of goats lived near the lake. Then local hunters discovered a big market for goatskin rugs, and wealthy Easterners and European noblemen came for sport, and a bloody slaughter began at Lake Chelan and throughout the range. Extinction of the goats seemed a very real possibility and therefore in 1925 hunting was prohibited in Washington.

The bands grew steadily for two decades and by the 1940s passengers on the Chelan-Stehekin boat regularly saw 100 or 200 goats on the cliffs. During

A visit from the landlord alongside the Blue Glacier, Olympic National Park

Mountain goats on side of Mt. Angeles

that period I hardly ever went on a climb in the Cascades without seeing at least a few and once counted 60 on Glacier Peak.

In 1948 the Washington State Game Department decided there were enough goats that shooting could start again and each year since has issued some 900 permits. In theory only about 300 are killed and the Game Department's periodic surveys purport to show the population is stable. Maybe so. But nowadays I rarely see a goat outside a national park. And passengers on the Lake Chelan boat see not hundreds but, if they have binoculars and are lucky, a half dozen.

The "boat count" is much more meaningful than the official survey. So is the count by the owners of a dude ranch in the southern Cascades. For 30 years they led guests (non-hunters) through the same portion of the Goat Rocks Wilderness during the same week in September. Before shooting resumed in 1948 they saw hundreds of goats on every trip. In 1972 they saw three. In 1973, none. They know why. In the 1950s they witnessed three hunters standing on a ridge crest shooting into a large band in a meadow basin below. The "sportsmen" kept banging away until they ran out of targets, then went down to the basin and from among their 20 kills picked the 3 best trophies. Three permits issued, 20 goats dead, many wounded.

Mountain goats on side of Mt. Angeles

The number of permits has no relation to the number killed. Even hunters who aren't mass-murderers see nothing wrong in shooting a second goat to replace the one they couldn't retrieve on an inaccessible cliff, or that in a long fall broke its horns and become worthless as a trophy. I have a friend who found one of the rare, friendly non-park goats; he confesses without pride that he walked to within 20 feet of the animal before shooting.

Possibly the official surveys are accurate and there were as many goats in the Cascades in 1974 as in 1964, or 1954. But perhaps the Game Department's 1947 count, that provided the baseline for judging the impact of hunting on the goat population, was far too low. If this is the case, later counts, more complete, would erroneously indicate a stable population. I'm almost certain there are fewer goats now. I know for sure they're warier. Unlike deer, goats learn to fear man or they don't live long. Where hunted they let themselves be seen only if they can't help it. Until recently there were non-park areas so remote the goats were still friendly. But then came the helicopter to carry gunners everywhere. Though the practice is strictly illegal, the goats are scouted from the air and, if rumors are true, sometimes are shot from the air.

I think it's high time to prohibit goat hunting for good. The Game Department's theory that they would multiply without limit and overgraze their range, as do deer, is nonsense. The thousands of goats inhabiting the Lake Chelan region in the 1890s were in balance with their habitat—which included abundant cougar and other predators to take care of any surplus. Protect the goats *and* the predators and they'll get along very well with the land—and with man. If there are not enough predators, the population should be controlled by the land manager in a humane way that will not permanently terrorize the remaining animals.

Hikers and climbers love to catch a glimpse of goats and marvel at their graceful skill on cliffs. Hunters love to shoot goats and saw off their heads for trophy-room walls. I am not opposed to all hunting. In fact, I have some very good friends who are ardent hunters, have a deep appreciation of wildlife, and are as concerned for conservation as I am. They have pointed out to me that just as the mountain goat is the symbol of mountain hikers, the goat is also the ultimate challenge to the hunter. However, I don't see the justice of denying 200,000 Washington backpackers a chance to enjoy such a magnificent animal so 900 hunters a year can enjoy their sport.

Mountain goats above the Athabaska River, Jasper National Park

Caribou near Polychrome Pass, Mt. McKinley National Park

Air view of caribou herd in the Talkeetna Mountains of Alaska

CARIBOU

The photographer's best friend in Mt. McKinley National Park is the caribou. At least, my twin brother Bob has this story to tell:

Near Polychrome Pass, 40 miles into the park from headquarters, my companion and I drove by this patriarch nibbling lichen a couple hundred yards up an open ravine. Quickly we popped out of the camper and sneaked within 200 feet of the animal. There was hardly a bush for cover but he was busy eating and pretended not to see us.

He browsed upward onto a tiny knoll against the skyline. We maneuvered to get him with a background of distant peaks. Our desires were of no interest to him. At last, feeling rejected, we just stood up and followed him around.

Suddenly we saw he was grazing *toward* us! My problem now became tactical retreat to fit him in the frame of the 200mm lens of my 35mm Nikon. Never guessing we'd have more than a snapshot or two of his tail, I'd taken off with only the telephoto on the camera and one extra roll of high-speed Ektachrome in my pocket. As I reloaded, Handsome chewed patiently.

For an hour we alternated—now we followed the buck, now he followed us. Sometimes I got the parked camper in the background, sometimes the valley or a vividly-colored cliff and snowy peak. Once my companion and I lined up so we were shooting at each other with the caribou between.

Finally Mr. Buck assumed a proud, statuesque stance on a hillock before the colorful peak. I sat down on soft moss, rested the heavy 200mm mount on my knees, and shot away as he turned his velvety rack whichever way I motioned (I'm *sure*). When he realized I'd shot the last frame on

my last 36-exposure roll he gave a friendly nod and headed uphill to greener pastures.

Travel brochures don't promise a look at Mt. McKinley—it's in clouds more than half the time. But summer bus tours leaving the hotel daily at 4 a.m. virtually guarantee game sightings. Fox, moose, Dall sheep, and (distant) Toklat grizzlies are usually seen. Caribou are nearly inevitable, maybe as scattered singles or, in autumn, small family groups. But many years there are unpredictable migrations when they sweep through the lower passes by the thousands in full view of the park road.

Certain areas of the park, especially Sable Pass, are posted for not leaving your car, or not leaving the road, partly so tourists won't chase the game away but mostly so grizzlies won't chase the tourists.

In recent years private conveyances haven't been allowed on the park road beyond Savage River except to drive to and from a designated campground, for which a permit is secured at park headquarters. Otherwise travel is by tour bus or free and frequent shuttle busses which stop a few minutes at all viewpoints.

I shot the photo of the caribou herd while leaning out the drafty back door of a twin-engine amphibian Goose operated by the U.S. Fish and Wildlife Service. For a month in midsummer of 1954 I flew from Anchorage with biologists surveying migrations of the Nelchina caribou herd and of salmon in the Copper River Basin. We'd wind along tributaries up to headwaters in alpine meadows, flying low enough to count (honestly) the bright red fish, then suddenly zoom over hilltops to follow the caribou. There were over 1000 in this little segment of the herd, here seen on a ridge of the Talkeetna Mountains southeast of McKinley.

Marmots in Edith Creek Basin, Mt. Rainier National Park

Pika drying hay for winter storage in the proposed Gros Ventre Wilderness, Wyoming

Marmot at Ipsut Pass, Mt. Rainier National Park

MARMOT AND PIKA

Marmots and pikas are as much a part of alpine meadows as lupine and paintbrush, and are seen by hikers nearly as often.

The pika, or conie, a chipmunk-size rodent, is a small animal with a large shrill voice. It lives in rockslides having lots of passageways for quick escapes. Harvey Manning tells of standing a half-hour in a field of granite boulders watching a pika dodge in and out of spaces between rocks, pursued by two weasels. None of the three paid any attention to Harvey but when his dog arrived they scattered. The pika is an industrious grass harvester. Search the area around its home and invariably you'll find small piles of hay drying on rocks. When fully cured the hay is stowed in underground "barns," the food supply for a long mountain winter.

The marmot, biggest of the rodent family, is famous for its human-like whistle, a warning to other marmots that danger is approaching. The first time I heard one was when Bob and I were hiking with Dad in the Olympics. We had a good laugh because Dad thought it was another hiker and whistled back.

The marmot is a burrower, typically tunneling a home under a boulder where it can't easily be dug out by coyotes, bears, and other creatures with a taste for marmot steaks. Most of its life seems to be spent sleeping, hibernating from September to June, sunning on boulders in the summer. Obviously they have to wake up once in a while. I've seen them carrying hay and stacking neat piles to dry. I watched one nibble down a complete patch of lupine, eating blossoms and all.

36

Marmot feasting on lupine near Panorama Point, Mt. Rainier National Park

Outside national parks marmots tend to be wary. Though they are legally protected, hunters think their whistling alerts deer and gun them down. A hiker may hear a whistle and after a long study of the terrain spot the whistler perched on a boulder-top lookout, blending into the background. Move in that direction and it dives for a burrow. Inside parks the marmot ignores humans, only ducking from sight when its immediate domain is invaded.

For a book on Rainier I spent much of a day photographing marmots in Edith Creek Basin, especially a youngster. Every time I moved a few feet toward him, he moved off a few feet. I tried talking, singing, even looking the other way while I angled around but he kept always just beyond good camera range. After taking a few pictures I sat down to change film and was so engrossed in the camera I didn't see the entire episode that followed. Evidently the little fellow had been so intent on watching me he didn't watch where he was going and ended up in the territory of a larger marmot.

There was a squealing and a sudden flurry. I looked up and the little marmot was running straight at me with the big bully on his tail. The little guy brushed right past me but when 5 feet away the big one spotted me, abruptly stopped, and scampered to his hole. I'm sure the little marmot ran to me knowing I'd scare off the bully. He lay down panting. I didn't have the heart to chase him anymore.

There are several kinds of marmots. The hoary and the yellow-bellied live in the Cascades. The mountains of Vancouver Island and the Olympic Peninsula have their own species evolved during the Ice Age, when isolated by a sea of glaciers from the rest of the Northwest.

37

Moose near the mouth of Pelican Creek, Yellowstone National Park

Moose are often seen at sunset at Shoshone Lake, Yellowstone National Park

In the Gros Ventre Range, Wyoming

In Yellowstone National Park

MOOSE

The place to see moose is the Canadian Rockies. Or rather it was when the Banff-Jasper Highway was a winding, rutted, dirt road only a fool would drive faster than 30 miles an hour. In those days we always saw moose, and lots of them. Now the highway is wide, paved, and fast and the odds of glimpsing one are about even.

My first experience was on the old road along the Assiniboine River. We spotted a bull in a field and I grabbed my camera and closed in. The field was a bit marshy but a small (well-trampled) knoll gave a good vantage point. I'd taken several shots when the bull started my way, finally getting so close I fled to the car. He wasn't really mad—I just happened to be standing on his bed. When he reached the knoll he promptly lay down.

Occasionally we've seen moose from the road in Yellowstone. Near the Yellowstone River my brother Bob hit a bonanza of three bulls bedded down and got all kinds of pictures.

While hiking the Granite Creek trail in the Gros Ventre Wilderness of Wyoming, we met a young moose grazing. He gave us a disdainful look and went on chomping. However, while seeming to ignore us he worked his way into the woods and once hidden by trees ran off. Later, in camp, my daughter Vicky looked up from her book and saw a bull splashing in the river. By the time she found me he was gone, of course.

Moose wading the Athabaska River, Jasper National Park

With a name longer than it is, a Cascades golden-mantled
ground squirrel plays hide-and-seek in an old stump on Spencer
Butte, Gifford Pinchot National Forest, Washington

Gentian, Grand Teton National Park

Cascades golden-mantled ground squirrel in Crater Lake National Park

CHIPMUNK AND SQUIRREL

The antics of chipmunks and squirrels have tickled millions of national park visitors, many of whom never see any wildlife close up except those friendly rodents. The little critters become beggars, hardly proper for park animals. But I confess that in weak moments I, too, have donated bits of lunch to ever-expanding cheeks.

In preparation for a rainy day the industrious creatures carry cheekload after cheekload of salted peanuts, bread crumbs, and other tidbits to private hoards. However, tourists are also around with handouts on rainy days and chipmunks and squirrels hibernate most of the winter so probably few peanuts ever are actually eaten. When Paradise Inn at Mt. Rainier ultimately is torn down, workmen undoubtedly will find enormous caches hidden in the walls and under the floors.

I suppose I most enjoy encounters in the forest, though I sort of resent an undeserved scolding from high in a tree as I wearily climb a steep hill. I'm also unhappy when a critter chews a hole in my pack and nibbles my chocolate, cheese, and crackers, not to mention my "squirrel food," a mixture of nuts, raisins, and candy I carry for trail snacks. But for every scolding and burglary there are a dozen incidents of curious eyes peeking from behind a tree, keeping just out of sight, and of tiny beasts surprised while tearing cones apart to get at the seeds which are their natural food.

In our yard at home we have both chipmunks and squirrels. Now and then the squirrel does a tightrope walk from the telephone pole to our house. Toward the middle the wire gets a bit shaky and often he has to hold on for dear life. Once he slipped and hung upside down a minute before climbing on top again. Another time he made it two-thirds of the way across, lost his nerve, and turned back.

The chipmunk is our most faithful neighbor. He (or she) stuffs his cheek pouches at our bird feeder and hides the loot in the garage. If the feeder is empty he sits on the edge staring at the kitchen window until someone comes out with a new supply.

44

COYOTE

Considering the vast number roaming the Northwest, I've seen surprisingly few coyote. Once in a great while I've glimpsed one at the edge of a road waiting for a chance to dash across. Generally they're well-hidden and camouflaged in grass and brush and don't make a public appearance unless sure they can escape to privacy in a hurry. Perhaps winter is the best season to see them, contrasted against the snow.

Speaking of predators, in all the time I've spent in the woods I've never seen a single cougar. Tracks, yes—on our honeymoon Pat and I discovered a big paw print in a small patch of snow 50 feet from our tent. Obviously the cougar had visited in the night because the print wasn't there when we went to bed. I don't feel so bad about cougar—Pat's father, who grew to manhood in genuine wilderness, during his whole life has seen only one.

Although wolves are often said to be extinct in Washington, I think I saw one in the North Cascades. I'd hiked up a trail-less ridge to timberline on the northeast side of Mt. Baker. After getting my pictures I sat down to change film. Suddenly the wolf walked from behind a tree. We saw each other at the same time. I hastily shoved the film into the camera but the animal disappeared. Of course it might have been a wild dog, but it matched pictures I've seen of wolves—short ears, large head, and at least twice as big as a coyote.

Among Pat's and my most memorable experiences with wildlife was a night spent with coyotes, years ago on a winter trip to Jackson Hole in Wyoming. We slept in our old station wagon, brilliant moonlight reflecting the snow, choirs of coyotes serenading all around. In the morning a pack crossed the road in front of us. That day we watched them as they sat watching the feeding lot, apparently waiting for the sicklier of the 15,000 or more elk to die.

The relationship between man and coyote has had ups and downs over the years. In the mythology of Northwest Indians the most admired figure was Old Coyote, wily and smart, full of mischief and fun, always outwitting his foes and playing tricks. He was also man's special friend, responsible (like Loki in Norse mythology and Prometheus in the Greek) for stealing fire from remote and selfish gods and giving it to the poor Indian, who until then shivered all winter and had to eat his fish raw.

Coyote tracks in the Stehekin valley, North Cascades National Park

The white man has been a biased judge of the coyote and summary executioner without trial. Actually, whatever sins the coyote may commit are far out-weighed by its virtues. If coyotes weren't handy to control them, the rabbit, gopher, and meadow mice populations would overrun the land—much to the sorrow of the ranchers who persecute coyotes with guns and poison.

Truth will out. Increasingly the coyote is gaining friends to protect him from the ignorance of ranchers. There never really has been any danger of totally exterminating this ingenious and adaptable creature, just of reducing its numbers and making it more wary. Aside from its value in the ecological scheme of things, I'm glad to see the coyote making a comeback. There's no more beautiful music in the wilderness than a coyote song. If the situation keeps improving, one of these years I may even get a good picture.

Pat had a wonderful chance for pictures once—if only she'd had a camera handy. While I was taking pictures of Mt. Olympus from near the top of a high ridge, Pat left her pack with me and wandered up to the crest and sat down. She'd only been there a few minutes when two coyote puppies came tumbling into view on the back side of the ridge, highlighted by a shaft of sun beaming down on them. She sat still and the two pups were so engrossed in play they didn't see her, even though they came within a hundred feet. There was no way Pat could let me know what was going on because if she moved the pups would spot her. Ten minutes later, when I'd finished my pictures, I went up the hill to join her and inadvertently scared the pups away. My only glimpse was two furry creatures disappearing behind a clump of trees.

Coyote in Lamar Valley, Yellowstone National Park

Wintertime in the Hoh rain forest, Olympic National Park,
where coyote tracks are often seen

PRONGHORN ANTELOPE

The pronghorn, perhaps the most beautiful animal in the United States, also is reputed to be the fastest, having been clocked at 60 miles an hour.

I'm a bit disillusioned with the old song, "Where the deer and the antelope play." To be sure, there are places where deer and antelope associate, but as a rule their habitats are miles apart. The deer graze close to a forest where they can spend the midday hours lying in the shade and hiding from enemies. The antelope prefers the "lone prairie" miles from the nearest tree where he can see and run from his enemies.

It's hard to miss antelope on the open plains of the Intermountain West. Traveling from Rocky Mountain National Park on Interstate 80 between Laramie and Rock Spring, we saw more than 100, scattered in twos and threes, sometimes mingling with cattle. Driving U.S. 40 in Utah, we saw from a distance what we thought were three cows with their heads hanging over the fence, watching the cars go by. When we discovered they were antelope we stopped, but they dashed off before I could focus the camera.

The best place to see numerous antelope is Yellowstone National Park, near Gardiner, where a large herd winters along the west valley road inside the park boundary. Seeing and photographing are two different things. Antelope don't pay much attention to a moving car but as soon as it stops, away they go. We drove the west valley road one summer morning just to see what the winter range looked like without snow. Dumb us. We didn't have cameras ready. Six antelope were feeding beside the road but by the time our cameras were out they were too far. How were we to know antelope occasionally use their winter range in summer?

My best luck came at Malheur Bird Refuge in Oregon, where biologists maintain a feeding lot for their studies. The antelope weren't tame so I put on a telephoto lens and got some nice distant shots. Then I had to change film. When I was ready to shoot again the animals were so close I could hardly focus. Naturally I'd left my normal lens in the car. I like to show the whole animal to prove that it isn't stuffed or in a cage, so I just knew these head shots wouldn't be any good but wasted two exposures anyway. I was half right. One film was worthless. The other is on the opposite page.

Pronghorn antelope in the National Bison Range, Montana

Pronghorn antelope in the Malheur National Wildlife Refuge, Oregon

BIGHORN SHEEP

One May I wandered up the lower slopes of Mt. Everts, just inside Yellowstone Park's Mammoth Hot Springs entrance, where a herd of a hundred bighorn sheep winters. I found part of the herd, a group of ewes and lambs, and got fairly close. Nobody being nearby to hear me, I sang to them. They seemed to like one song about as much as another. Though never applauding, they sort of accepted me and grazed all around the spot I was sitting. The trouble was I ran out of film before they were close enough for the really great pictures I could have taken had I waited. I've had other chances in Yellowstone for sheep pictures. There is generally a herd near the fire lookout on Mt. Washburn. However, usually too many people are around for me to try a serenade.

While walking along the Garden Wall in Glacier National Park, my wife Pat and I spotted four large rams above the trail. We dropped packs and stealthily crept upward, almost within camera range. Then two teenage boys came noisily running. We were furious. However, the sheep went on grazing and the boys walked right up to them. Pat and I abandoned our stalking and walked up to the sheep too.

They're not always so nonchalant. My old friend, the late Jack Hazle, used to tell of the time he was climbing a peak in Glacier Park and suddenly suffered a barrage of rockfall. He knew the mountains there are rotten but couldn't figure why this one was disintegrating for no apparent reason—until he saw a big ram on a ledge above, deliberately kicking off rubble with his rear legs. Jack chose another route up the cliff.

Bighorn are scattered throughout the Rocky Mountains—nowadays mainly in the parks. As early as 1832 the white man began his slaughter. In that year Captain B. L. E. Bonneville led a band of 14 trappers into Stanley Basin, now a part of Idaho's Sawtooth National Recreation Area and being studied for inclusion in a national park. They found sheep abundant in the precipices and so friendly the men could easily surround them and kill as many as they pleased—which was a lot. Only a handful survive in the Sawtooths and they are almost never seen by tourists.

Attempts are being made to transplant the animals back to their original habitats in other

Bighorn sheep in Yellowstone National Park

Bighorn sheep on Mt. Washburn, Yellowstone National Park

parts of the West, such as northeast Washington and the Cascades. Eight sheep were planted in a huge enclosure in Lava Beds National Monument in northern California. The enclosure was near the road and thousands of visitors enjoyed the two magnificent rams and their harem of six ewes. However, in the fall of 1973 two "sportsmen" shot the rams and cut off their heads. They were caught lifting the bloody "trophies" over the fence.

Several varieties of bighorn, including the desert sheep and the rimrock bighorn, have lost so much of their habitat to civilization and have been so overhunted they are close to extinction. The few left in the High Sierra are unable amid the hordes of hikers to find the privacy they want during their breeding season and therefore aren't maintaining their numbers. Authorities are considering placing some areas off-limits to people.

Overleaf: Bighorn sheep near the Garden Wall trail, Glacier National Park

51

Buffalo in the Lamar Valley, Yellowstone National Park

BUFFALO

I've become a firm believer in taking buffalo pictures near a handy tree and preferably with a companion.

On one of my many winter trips to Yellowstone I saw a big bull near Old Faithful and made a respectfully wide swing around the beast to get a good angle. I just had the camera focused when he started walking away. Then he turned and headed in my direction. Okay, I thought, I'm on a path he wants to use. No argument. I moved aside. But *that* wasn't the problem because he immediately veered toward me.

I decided it was time to aim my skis at a friendly tree. I looked back and he was running. That did it. I kicked off the skis and scrambled into the branches. As soon as I began climbing the bull stopped running. He leisurely circled the tree, then wandered off. I stayed up there a good half-hour, until he was completely out of sight. Believe me, it wouldn't have been half as lonesome if I'd brought a companion.

I related my experience to a ranger who said the previous week he, too, had been chased up a tree. But he was in more of a hurry and didn't have time to take off his skis. He must have been using a very special wax.

Buffalo are best seen in winter or early spring in Yellowstone National Park. A hundred or so winter in the Lamar Valley and about that many along the Firehole River. To reach feed they plow away snow by swinging their massive heads.

Actually, the rangers don't consider the buffalo extremely dangerous. They don't suggest trying to be chummy but say few people have been seriously hurt—though one man was

Buffalo feeding along the Firehole River

killed. If a buffalo takes out after a person it will knock him down, but having proven who is master, will walk away. He won't try to gore or trample a victim.

The same is true of buffalo fighting buffalo. Unless the other guy puts up a scrap, the aggressor doesn't push the quarrel. As is the case with many animals, the instinct for survival is stronger than anger. They don't really want to get involved in an all-out battle. It wastes too much energy needed for survival. Also, even the winner could get seriously hurt. A buffalo just wants to show who's boss, and as long as no one contests him, leaves well enough alone.

It's strange we Americans are so shocked by the African tribesmen decimating the last wild herds of their continent. We were far better educated and far better fed when we came within an inch of exterminating our buffalo. We should lend our money and time and sympathy to helping prevent the slaughter of African animals. Yes, we should find it sad. But shocking, no.

Overleaf: Buffalo at Beach Springs thermal area, Yellowstone National Park

Bear near Lake Wenatchee in the Washington Cascades

BEAR

Everybody has bear stories. Tell your favorite and someone is sure to top you. Each summer we see four or five bear, usually with no exciting story resulting because mainly they ignore us—partly due to eyesight so notoriously poor that if hikers are quiet the bear often don't even know they're being watched. A decent distance makes for happiness all around. We already have plenty of stories and don't mind their rudeness in not paying us more attention.

Only one time have I met a bear who showed active dislike for me and seemed on the point of doing something about it. He was eating blueberries a hundred feet off the Golden Lakes trail in Mt. Rainier National Park. As I passed he growled. *That's* a sound I don't care if I ever hear again. My hair stood on end but there was no choice except to keep walking and pray.

Bears love berries. Once my mother was out with a neighbor harvesting a special blackberry patch near home. Mother heard the neighbor pulling at vines on the other side of a thicket and talked to her while picking. No answer. Finally Mother walked around the thicket to see why her friend wouldn't talk. That was no friend, that was a bear. Mother was in such a rush to get away she spilt half her berries.

Most of our stories are about "civilized" bear, the ones that have lost their fear of man and learned he carries all sorts of good things to eat. My first encounter was in the 1920s, in Yellowstone. I remember Dad and the other campers banging away on pots and pans to scare a bear out of Old Faithful Campground.

Nowadays park rangers are installing garbage cans that are (hopefully) bearproof and trying to teach tourists to make themselves the same by not being traveling supermarkets. Gradually the "campground bear" is becoming less of a menace. But there are lots of vivid memories of the bear-ier past. Once Harvey Manning took his two oldest daughters, Penny and Becky, then 6 and 4 years old, camping at Rainier. The girls were up at the crack of dawn looking for amusement and Harvey, wanting more sleep, told them to go away and leave him alone. "What shall we do?" they asked. "Oh," said he gruffly, "Go chase a bear." A bit later he was wakened by screams and laughs and running feet. Penny and Becky returned yelling gleefully, "Daddy! Daddy! We found a bear and chased him and he ran up a tree!" Harvey decided he'd had enough sleep.

Robber bears by no means stick to campgrounds. In our Boy Scout days my brother Bob was left in charge of a tentful of food at the road while the rest of us relayed loads up the trail to our camp at Lena Lake. Bob was inside the tent when a bear ripped open the back. As bruin entered the new back door, Bob went out the old front door.

On the way to climb Mt. Olympus, Bob and his wife Norma and I cached food and spare clothing in a bag hung from rafters of the Hoh Lake Shelter. On our return the bag was gone. We had some mighty evil thoughts about thieving fishermen, but soon had to mentally apologize. Gathering firewood, we discovered our stuff slashed and chewed and strewn down the hill below the shelter. We salvaged what food we could and found all the clothes except Norma's extra shoes. Either there was a bear that wore shoes or a hungry one that ate leather.

While doing a story on the Ranger at the Olympus Guard Station I visited the little house out back. It had a tilt that kept the door from shutting. On my return the ranger, Louie Kirk, made a visit. He came back disgruntled, wanting to know what I'd done to the toilet paper. I said I'd used some but otherwise was innocent of any misdeed. Louie continued to make accusations so we all went to examine the evidence. In the few minutes between my visit and his, a bear had pulled the door open and bit the toilet roll. We peeled off the part he'd slobbered up but his teeth marks cut clear to the center. I decided I'd hate to have those jaws clamp down on my arm or leg.

I thought that might happen the night I was sacked out alone at Paradise Campground on Rainier. My dreams were disturbed by something rustling the sleeping bag. Then the Something *stepped* on me and just like that I was wide awake. I sat straight up—and was eyeball to eyeball with a great big black bear. Well, maybe it was only a *little* bear but it definitely was more bear than I wanted breathing in my face. Fortunately he felt the same about me and got the heck out in a hurry.

Bear track on the Hoh River trail, Olympic National Park

That was my second-closest call.

While still newlyweds Pat and I were camping near Jasper in the Canadian Rockies with a group of Mountaineers. In the evening she and I drove to the garbage dump to watch the bear. There were at least a dozen, and an equal number of tourists. The tourists were really dumb—rolling down car windows a couple inches and feeding bear through the slots. How stupid! Those huge bear were perfectly capable of smashing the windows if they felt the tourists weren't handing out goodies fast enough. I was too smart for that. Whenever a bear came close I drove away. Better safe than sorry. Only I got so fascinated watching bear in front of the car I didn't see the one that came from behind—until suddenly he reared up and, just to get my attention, stuck a paw through my wide-open window and slapped my face.

In nothing flat I had the car moving. Pat wiped the mud off my face. Underneath were red scratches. Back in camp our Mountaineer friends were curious. Somebody asked why Pat and I had been fighting. I insisted those weren't the marks of my bride's fingernails, I swore a bear did it. To this day, though, you hear stories in some circles about the lovers' quarrel Pat and I had.

Bear cubs begging alongside the Banff-Jasper Highway, Banff National Park

Lake of the Hanging Glacier, on the upper edge of bear country, Purcell Range, British Columbia

Porcupine at Cottonwood Campground, Entiat Valley, North Cascades of Washington

PORCUPINE

Way back when I was courting Pat we were spending a day in the country with her folks. During lunch we heard an uproar in the woods—barking, howling, yelping. Pat's father, the old wilderness hand, knew the sound. "Dog after a porky," he said. Sure enough, we investigated and found a large retriever harassing a little porcupine. The fool dog looked like a pincushion for all the quills in its snout but wouldn't quit. Even as we watched, the porcupine gave its quill-bristling tail a quick flip, slapping the dog in the face.

Soon the dog's owner showed up, equipped with a pair of pliers, and sadly explained this wasn't the first time. It was the *third*. We helped hold the dog while the quills were pulled. What pain! You'd think a dog would learn. Many never do, though, and that's something hikers who take man's best friend in the wilderness should think about.

I had a terrible fright hiking the Ingalls Creek trail at dusk, the light so dim I had to stare at the ground to place my feet. By pure chance I looked up—and a couple feet away, at eye level, was a porcupine gnawing bark of a pine tree. I easily could have come within slapping distance of that tail.

The porcupine is a frustrating beast, so smug about its defenses that it's completely fearless, and will poke around a camp, into packs, paying no attention to shouts. What can a hiker do? Well, in daytime you can prod a porky away with a stick. Nights are the problem.

One September Harvey Manning climbed a trail in the Cascades to the top of Surprise Mountain, which then had a fire lookout cabin on the summit. The youth stationed in the lookout came to meet him and in a state of near hysteria babbled out a terrible story. Every night since June porcupines had been crawling up on the cabin roof and chewing the cedar shakes. He hadn't had a good night's sleep in months. The crunching-crunching-crunching was driving him crazy.

Skunks at Toleak Point, Olympic National Park

SKUNK

What would *you* do if you found yourself 5 feet from a skunk you'd caught eating your lunch? Well, I didn't do anything either.

I'd often "encountered" skunks before, smelling where they'd been, seeing their cute little tracks on beach sands, but because they are mainly nocturnal, seldom had had a look at one. On this trip, though, in broad daylight we'd seen a half-dozen near Toleak Point, on the Olympic National Park Ocean Strip, pulling apart piles of seaweed in search of whatever they consider delicacies. Not having a telephoto lens with me, for obvious reasons I didn't get close enough for good, sharp pictures. (If you've ever noticed, *most* skunk pictures are fuzzy.)

That night, camped on the beach a short way from the point, I woke up to discover a hole freshly chewed in our tent. I flicked on a flashlight just in time to see a skunk dragging off a 6-inch salami. That's a lot of salami to give up without a fight. I scrambled out of sleeping bag and tent and into the driftwood. There he was, chomping our lunch, paying no more attention to my flashlight than an actor on a stage. I spoke a few soft words of protest, made a few half-hearted gestures, but he completely ignored me. I finally decided on the same course of action and went back to bed.

When you've got the Bomb, why worry? That's the motto of the skunk. Rare is the hiker so ignorant he doesn't show proper respect. If the little guy turns his back on you and lifts his tail, look out! Still another reason for not taking dogs in the wilderness is that they have to learn the hard way, and dog owners tell me it's a really heartbreaking business. Your buddy doesn't understand what he's done wrong, why your love suddenly has turned to hate. He was just trying to do his job of protecting his master. It hurts his feelings when he jumps in your lap and you yell and cough and shove him off.

SEA LION

Have you ever been told off by a hundred sea lions? I have. It's eerie and deafening. But I guess I had it coming.

I was working on a picture story of Redwood National Park, which everyone knows contains magnificent trees but few realize also has a beautiful shoreline. Perhaps the best way to enjoy the views of beach and ocean is by walking the Coast Trail that wanders along the top of a 600-foot cliff. Among the attractions, sea lions can be heard and, with luck, seen swimming in the sea or lying on offshore rocks.

The sea lions raise their young on Castle Rock, just north of Crescent City. In the course of their wanderings they even swim up the Klamath River several miles looking for eels and smelt. But I'd heard that in their spare time they also sun themselves on remote beaches, and that's what interested me. Hiking the Coast Trail one day, sure enough, there they were on rocks amid the surf.

I scrambled down the brushy cliff—and soon noted the shiny leaves I was slithering through were poison oak. Fortunately I wasn't hiking in shorts as I usually do, but in long pants. I put on parka and mittens and kept going.

I ended up on a promontory about a hundred feet from the lions. They paid me no attention and I shot up a lot of film. Several favorite rocks were so crowded there wasn't any space left empty. So, when a newcomer climbed on he'd have to push off, of bluff off, an animal already there. Often they'd both fall off. When the newcomer had a foothold he'd crawl over the mass of sleeping bodies and squirm into a niche. In the process he'd wake up lions who'd stir and grumble and flop back to sleep.

In moving to a different vantage point I got too close and spooked them. All at once and all together they set up an unbelievable din and plunged into the sea, forming a semicircle below me and yapping for everything they were worth. In fact, they were still yapping a half-hour later as I climbed back through the poison oak to the Coast Trail.

Steller sea lions, Redwood National Park. Below they are expressing their opinion of me.

Quillayute Needles at Olympic National Park's Second Beach,
where starfish and sea anemones and many other creatures are
found in the intertidal zone

WHALE

There's an old song about a whale of a tale, and truly a tail of a whale can make a whale of a tale.

Whales aren't commonly seen by landlubbers but we occasionally spot them while hiking the Olympic National Park Ocean Strip. One day we saw four from the beach at LaPush. Next day, north of the Quillayute River, a larger whale poked his head from the water, slowly made a 180-degree turn, looking at the beach, and submerged.

When whales come up for air they blow off columns of spray that can be seen from a considerable distance, most easily from a bluff high above the water. One time I was taking surf pictures from Portage Head, north of the Park Ocean Strip, when nature called. I discreetly left my companions and sought privacy behind a large tree. While there I saw a whale and yelled, "Look at the whale!" Me and my big mouth. Me and my dumb companions. Instead of enjoying the view from where they were they came running to my hideaway. I was pretty busy for a minute.

Whales migrate south in fall and north in spring and during these seasons often are observed in large pods. They seem to spend a few weeks off Grays Harbor on the Washington coast. One year a friend who runs a charter service at Westport invited me out to photograph whales. Well, we certain saw a lot, some very close to the boat, but it was futile trying to get pictures. They were surfacing all around but always were gone before I could focus. Anyhow, I saw quite a few tails of whales.

The tail of a whale near Westport, Washington

Salmon leaping a cascade in the Soleduck River, Olympic National Park

SALMON

While walking to grade school in Shelton I'd stop on the bridge across Goldsbough Creek to watch the endless flow of salmon going upstream to spawn. The more daring kids would try to grab a few. I don't remember any success, which is lucky because it was illegal. Oldtimers said what we saw was nothing, that once there'd been truly *big* salmon runs, the rivers so solid with fish there was no room left for the water.

It used to be exciting to watch Indians dip salmon below Celilo Falls on the Columbia River. That sight is long gone, thanks to Dalles Dam drowning the falls. Anyway, there aren't many salmon left in the Columbia. The series of dams makes their upstream passage difficult. And when the young fish are heading downstream to the ocean they get chewed up by turbines or poisoned by excess nitrogen churned into the water.

The solution to one problem leads to another problem. When Grand Coulee Dam was built for electricity and irrigation it forever blocked the upper Columbia to salmon migration, so hatcheries were built to perpetuate the fish artificially. One of these, at Leavenworth in the Cascades, gets its fresh water from mountain lakes which in the 1930s were dammed at outlets to raise their levels, making them into fluctuating reservoirs. There weren't many hikers then and the loss of a few of the hundreds of lakes in what now is proposed as the Alpine Lakes Wilderness didn't seem important. But today thousands of hikers are seeking out lakes like those that were ruined and not a single one could be called "surplus." If you live in the Northwest the destruction of Heart and Colchuck and Snow Lakes, and the several others that supply the Leavenworth hatchery, is part of the price of your electricity.

Among the best remaining spots to see salmon is the Soleduck Cascades in Olympic National Park. Each autumn for a couple weeks they make flying leaps at the small cascade. Watch a while and you recognize the same fish jumping time after time before surmounting the falls.

The salmon die after spawning, their carcasses gather in eddies and pools, and it's feasting season for bears and bald eagles. That's something we don't think about when arguing over who gets what share of fish. For example, the salmon that spawn on the Skagit River in Washington must first run the gantlet of commercial and sports fishermen and Indians exercising treaty rights. If any of these groups should take too many fish the bald eagles wintering near Marblemount would be in serious trouble.

So many fishermen compete with the ospreys and pelicans at the famous Fishing Bridge across Yellowstone River that the park reduced the limit to two fish per person. But every year more visitors bring fishing poles and if they all caught just one fish apiece the birds would starve.

To a greater or lesser extent, all fishing by man competes with wildlife. Their needs must be considered when setting fishing seasons.

Turtles in a marsh in eastern Washington

Red-winged blackbird in eastern Washington

American bittern in a small pond in eastern Washington

AMERICAN BITTERN

I was driving by a marsh in Eastern Washington and saw what I thought was a stick poking out of the water. But I wasn't sure and stopped the car and backed up for a second look. It was a bird standing motionless in the shallows with its long bill pointed straight up. I'd never heard of such a bird before but at last identified it as a male American bittern.

I watched a while and finally he lowered his head and stalked off. By observing the moving grass I occasionally got glimpses of him. He kept making the oddest noise, a sort of underwater "ker-punk."

There was a bit of commotion and out walked a female with a 6-inch fish thrashing in her bill. The male followed, intent on sharing the feast.

I didn't see who swallowed the fish because most of the action was hidden. My guess is she did. Anyway, once the fish was gone harmony was restored and both disappeared in the marsh, from which I continued to hear "ker-punk! ker-punk!"

MARSH BIRDS

The best and most portable bird-watching blind is a car parked beside a marsh. Unquestionably the greatest bird marshes in the Northwest are those at California's Tule Lake and Oregon's Malheur National Wildlife Refuges, but the Potholes area near Moses Lake in Washington is also good. For us the salt marsh on the shore of Puget Sound near the Edmonds ferry dock, a mile from our home, is a lot handier.

Summer and winter, marshes are apt to be noisy. Among my favorite residents are red-winged and yellow-headed blackbirds that feed off last year's cattails, and avocets, which have long legs for wading and long, slender bills with funny upturned bends for scooping up little creatures in the mud. Among my unfavorite wildlife at Malheur, and adding to the noise, are the clouds of mosquitoes. However, some of the birds love them.

Once when I'd stopped at a pond near Spokane to photograph red-winged blackbirds a turtle crawled out onto a sunny log. Before I could focus on it, a second one crawled out. They stayed just long enough for me to snap a picture and then slid back into the murky water.

American avocet in Potholes Reservoir, Washington

California quail in our backyard

House finch on a red-hot poker in our yard

QUAIL

A covey of California quail lives on and near our lot. Some years we've counted as many as 25 in the yard. Other times, after a population explosion among the neighborhood cats, we're lucky to keep a pair.

In nature the hunters and hunted stay in balance. The predator overkills, gets hungry, moves on, and the species he preys on build up again. But when a domestic cat or dog overkills and gets hungry he goes home to his Alpo or Purina Cat and Dog Chow—which, however, never satisfy his yearning for fresh raw meat. I like pets and understand why people own them but I enjoy wildlife more and you can't have both. I get furious when I look out the window and see a neighbor's cat leap on a quail and drag it off. I've invented ways to teach marauders not to mess around with my quail but there seems an endless supply of new ones that need a lesson.

During spring and early summer the covey splits up into pairs. It's quite a sight when they bring forth chicks. Often a family starts out with a dozen tiny butterballs that stumble over every little obstacle. Sadly, the families get steadily smaller as the cats do their work.

Generally a fair number survive, the males developing tiny topknots as they grow. In fall, when they all look adult, the scattered families rejoin forces to go through the winter as a united covey.

When raising a family, the male stands guard on a high perch while the female and chicks feed. We hear him giving instructions from our roof or telephone pole. One year two males lost their mates. They combined families, divided the chores, and did a good job of bringing up their young.

Quail are not tame. They tolerate us inside the house, unless we make a sudden movement, but spook when we go out. Usually they fly off when startled but several times we've watched a whole family or covey freeze, standing motionless in whatever positions they were when the alarm was given. Once we timed them in a freeze for 15 minutes. We never did see what caused their worry.

In our yard and an adjacent vacant lot are terrible tangles of blackberry vines that I really ought to clear out. I have a perfect excuse, though—they make ideal quail refuges. Often we hear them talking inside the tangles.

California quail feeding along our back fence

Red-breasted nuthatch   *Chipmunk*   *Hummingbird*

BACK YARD BIRDS

Our lot in Edmonds, 15 miles north of Seattle, isn't big but it's full of birds. My wife Pat has a feeder outside the kitchen window where we can watch them or, as we sometimes suspect, they can watch us. In season we're visited by Steller's jays, juncos, song sparrows, towhees, flickers, gold-crowned sparrows, house finches, and many many English sparrows. In summer the house finches and hummingbirds keep Pat busy filling the hummingbird feeder. She plants red-hot pokers which attract finches, hummingbirds, and an occasional western tanager. A family of goldfinches sits on our telephone wire 50 feet from the house, never coming closer. Pat puts out a suet-and-birdseed ball hung in a netting bag that's supposed to be especially for chickadees, bushtits, and red-breasted nuthatches but is also popular with starlings, Steller's jays, and flickers. Apple halves on the lawn draw robins and varied thrushes. Cedar waxwings stop by for a day or two in fall to join the robins in eating mountain ash berries.

Two residents of our yard who take care of their own food supply, darting through the air after flying bugs, are the barn swallow and violet-green swallow. When our son Johnny was a little boy he made birdhouses of indoor plywood. They'd have disintegrated in the wet winter so we took them in each fall, then put them out in spring before the swallows arrived. Two years in a row we were late and the swallows sat on the telephone line by the kitchen window, chirruping at us until we rushed out and put up their houses.

My favorite small bird is the chickadee, partly because they don't desert us in winter. I love their friendly chick-a-dee-dee-dee. I chick-a-dee-dee-dee back and occasionally even get an answer. Several families nest in our neighborhood, including one couple that some years uses our birdhouse. They're furtive when nesting, first flying into our big cedar tree, checking to make sure the coast is clear, then flying to the birdhouse. When heading out to look for food they also pause at the cedar.

Except when nesting they're very chummy, hopping around branches a couple of feet overhead, twittering, and chick-a-dee-dee-deeing down at me as I walk to the mailbox or work in the yard. They're so tiny and so constantly flitting, never sitting still more than a moment, I've never had any luck getting a picture in our back yard. However, I was more successful with the mountain chickadee in Yellowstone National Park.

Western grebes in Klamath Basin National Wildlife Refuges on the Oregon-California border, on the left with nest, on the right with baby

Snow geese in flight over the Skagit Wildlife Area, Washington

SNOW GOOSE

What a racket! I've never seen snow geese in anything but enormous flocks and the noise they make is overwhelming. From a mile away they look and sound like a huge hive of bees taking off. Close up the roar of a thousand wings and squawks is indescribable.

Over 10,000 snow geese winter on the Skagit Flats in Washington, an hour's drive from our home. Usually they're out in the salt marshes or on the water, inaccessible by foot or boat. Occasionally the marshes freeze and they descend on farmers' fields. That is the time to see them near at hand.

Twice I've been lucky enough to see the spring migration of 200,000 snow geese at Tule Lake, in the Klamath Basin National Wildlife Refuges on the Oregon-California border. Dikes and roads permit driving to easy views. Once Pat and I spent a moonlight night on the dikes (that is forbidden now), all night long listening to geese squabbling, now and then spooking and exploding into mass flight.

A couple times I've spooked them by inadvertently getting too close and they've disappeared over the horizon—or settled down a few hundred yards away. Other times they've spooked for no reason I could see, headed for some other pasture—or circled a few minutes and returned to the same spot. What bothers them I don't know.

Of course, there's no mystery about it in the shooting season, when hunters keep the flocks scattered. Like most outdoors people, I stay far away from the hunters. It's not just that their guns scare me. I get sad thinking of those magnificent birds becoming goose soup.

Man isn't the only enemy of the goose. Coyote, raccoons, and skunks take their toll. During December and January bald eagles feed on geese crippled and left to die by hunters. Between 3 to 7 million birds use the Klamath Basin in the fall. Nobody knows exactly how many are crippled by gunshot. Officials of the Klamath Basin National Wildlife Refuges claim the total is only about 250, but knowledgeable estimates range from 2500 to 25,000. Whatever the number, the cripples are now an important food source for predators.

Snow geese in the Klamath Basin National Wildlife Refuges

Overleaf: Uncountable snow geese over Tule Lake, Klamath Basin National Wildlife Refuges, California

PELICAN

The pelican is an ungainly creature. See one on the ground and you just know it can't possibly fly. In the air it looks like some prehistoric monster. But you gain a lot of respect when you watch it take a few powerful beats with its wings and then stretch into a long, easy glide.

As the poem says, a pelican's bill holds more than his belly can. After he gets a fish in his bill he may spend a half-hour juggling it around to get in position for swallowing. For all the grotesqueness—including an odd wart that develops on top of the bill of a mature male—in a weird sort of way the pelican is a beautiful bird, its wings having gleaming white feathers with a little black tip.

Pat and I have seen white pelicans in Eastern Oregon, California's Tule Lake, Yellowstone, and Ethiopia. On that last trip we'd driven into a bird refuge and parked. Though there wasn't a soul in sight, I locked the car. After a few minutes of shooting Pat went back to the car for film. To her consternation a half-dozen men, each with a long spear, were looking in the windows. She got so flustered she had a terrible time unlocking the car and then couldn't find the film. She gave up and rejoined me. When we returned to the car, men and spears were gone but one door was open. The only thing missing was my very old jacket, practically worthless to me but to the Ethiopians the sole article of any value. The thousand dollars worth of camera gear didn't interest them.

Previous page: Lower Green River Lake and Square Top Mountain in Bridger Wilderness, Wyoming, home not only of many birds but also elk and moose

Brown pelicans at the mouth of the Klamath River, Redwood National Park, preening, flying, and yawning

Brown pelican taking off near the mouth of the Klamath River,
Redwood National Park

*White pelicans soaring at the Hart Mountain National Antelope
Range, Oregon*

White pelicans at the Klamath Basin National Wildlife Refuges, Oregon-California border

Brown pelicans are frequent visitors to Redwood National Park. During summer months rangers leading nature walks count on seeing a few riding ocean swells just beyond the breakers. They also are found in the harbor at Crescent City and on the Klamath River bar. The pelicans of the redwoods country are immature. Mature birds spend summers nesting in the Channel Islands off the coast from San Diego.

Tragically, the pelican is in danger. Because of high concentrations of DDT, their egg shells are so thin they can't be hatched. Where thousands used to hatch in the Channel Islands, in recent years there've been only a dozen or less. The birds live 8 to 12 years, so many are still around, but when this generation is gone the beautiful, wonderful bird may no longer be seen in the redwoods area. Fortunately, the brown pelican so far seems to be doing better on the Mexican coast.

Mature white male pelicans develop a bump on their bills.

Trumpeter swans on Barney Lake near Mt. Vernon, Washington

TRUMPETER SWAN

From a distance only an expert can readily tell the difference between the whistling and trumpeter swans. Both are huge, with 6- to 7-foot wing spans, and both are all white with black beaks. The major differences are in the degree of blackness of their beaks and the sound of their voices.

A few trumpeter swans winter in the Skagit valley of Western Washington. When farm fields are flooded they can be seen from country roads. Otherwise they mainly appear as small dots on Barney Lake or nearby Clear Lake. Sad to say, though protected from hunting, many are dying, poisoned by eating lead birdshot.

Some swans make their permanent residence in Yellowstone National Park. In the summer a pair is often swimming on well-named Swan Lake. Naturally, the day of our visit they were on the far side. My daughter Vicky and I walked around, easy enough to do except for a long detour to avoid a swamp at the outlet, and got fairly close to the swans. Our feet being thoroughly wet, on the return we waded the outlet. It was deeper than it looked and we got our shirt tails wet too.

Trumpeter swan on Swan Lake, Yellowstone National Park

Canada geese feeding in the Firehole River. The air temperature was −20° and the water covered with fog.

Trumpeter swans in a backwater of the Yellowstone River near Livingston, Montana

Canada geese on the edge of the Columbia River near Puget City, Washington

CANADA GOOSE

Canada geese make an odd barking sound which has earned them their other name, "honkers." Though mainly migratory, they sometimes settle down and happily nest in the Northwest—in early summer it's exciting to watch a family on lakes in Eastern Washington. In spring they visit the Potholes near Moses Lake, as well as the larger reservoirs. In winter they can be seen at wildlife refuges and along the Firehole River in Yellowstone National Park.

Fifteen years ago, when we moved to our house in Edmonds, we often saw geese headed south in fall, flying in the classic V formation, and during the still of night heard the distinctive honking of flights passing overhead. I don't know why but nowadays we don't see many and seldom hear them. Maybe there are fewer birds, or we just don't look out the window as much. Or perhaps the rising din from freeways and airways has drowned out the honking.

Canada geese in formation near Moses Lake, Washington

Canada geese on shore of Banks Reservoir in Washington

Great blue heron photographed from car window along the Oregon coast

HERON

From childhood canoe trips I vividly remember heron, big awkward-looking birds that reminded me of pterodactyls, squawking overhead as they flew at sunset to roosts high in trees. For years since I've watched them around Puget Sound, frequently standing in shallow water waiting for a meal to swim by.

The great blue heron, a magnificent bird, is common in Redwood National Park and along the Oregon coast. It's very elusive, though, taking flight when you're still a quarter-mile away. Occasionally I've rounded a bend in a river and got within a hundred feet of one but by the time I focused the camera always it was gone.

For a book on Redwood National Park I thought I'd be clever and let the heron come to me, so I hid amid logs on a small island in tideflats at the mouth of the Klamath River. It was a good idea except for one thing—I misjudged how high the tide would be and when. I waded to the island through ankle-deep water but quickly was surrounded by angry surf. From 1 o'clock in the afternoon until 8 in the evening I was trapped, cold and hungry. And the water got so deep the heron never did show up.

I had better luck on Hood Canal when we spent the night in our camper parked by the beach. In the morning two heron were feeding just outside. I poked my camera out the back door and they flew off. Soon they returned, landing a bit in front of the camper. I snuck around and got one shot before they took off. Then, while driving away, I had my best chance and snapped two exposures from the truck window. Funny how scared they are of people but not of cars. Often they can be seen feeding beside a busy highway.

Great blue heron on Hood Canal, Washington   *Overleaf: Ptarmigan in summer dress, Glacier National Park*

Ptarmigan in winter dress, Mt. Rainier National Park

GROUSE AND PTARMIGAN

Grouse add a lot of spice to the mountain scene. In spring the cock's drumming can be heard for miles. In summer a hiker often meets hens with broods of chicks. In any season a person can have the wits scared out of him by an explosion beside the trail as a grouse takes to the air.

Three varieties of grouse live in Northwest mountains—spruce or Franklin's, ruffed, and blue. The drumming is the cock's springtime mating call. The ruffed grouse drums with its wings, making a slow, pounding noise that gets faster and faster, sounding like a distant motor starting. The others drum by use of special sacs on the sides of their necks, filling them with air to act as percussion instruments of a sort, and going "whoomp-whoomp-whoomp-wp."

The drumming also stakes a territorial claim. Years ago I was set up for a picture of Mt. Rainier when fog blew in. I waited for it to blow out. And waited. After several hours, with nothing to do, I began imitating a nearby grouse. He went "whoomp-whoomp-wp." I went "whoomp-whoomp-wp." It was a very interesting conversation. However, I should have had a translater to tell me what I was saying because all of a sudden

Previous page: Spruce grouse, a patient model, in Heather Meadows, Mt. Baker National Forest, Washington

the bird flew out of the fog straight at me. We saw each other at the same instant. He folded wings and dropped to the ground with a thud and sat there staring at me. I started whoomping again and he stood up. The red sacs on his neck puffed out, he gave a couple whoomps, and stalked off. I guess he decided he didn't care to tangle with any grouse as big as me. There were plenty of hens other places.

I was hiking with my daughter Vicky in the Wind River Range of Wyoming when we came upon a hen with a bunch of chicks. The chicks dove in the brush and froze. The mother spread her tail and invited me to chase her. However, I wanted grouse pictures, not grouse meat, and slipped off my pack to dig out the camera. But this meant I was staying right in the area where the chicks were hiding so mama decided more drastic action was needed. While I was bent over getting the camera, the darn bird flew up and attacked my rear. Between the hen's assaults and Vicky's laughter, it took me so long to set up the camera the bird took off before I could focus.

What the grouse is to forests and subalpine meadows, its cousin, the ptarmigan, is to tundras and snowfields higher in the mountains. They live in the arctic-alpine zones of Washington, Canada, Alaska, Siberia, and Japan. I've also seen them in Lapland. In Washington they're protected from hunting, but not in Alaska. In Scandinavia, where they are a staple part of the diet, the people chase them into nets and trap them.

The ptarmigan is one of the great camouflage experts, speckled brown and white in summer so it blends into heather and rocks, and except for a red eyebrow and black beak, pure white in winter, virtually impossible to see in snow. On a sunny day you may spot the shadow before seeing the bird. Generally they give themselves away by a chicken-like clucking. Or maybe it's just the noisy birds I see. As is also true of grouse, they're so confident of their camouflage they're fearless. Often a hiker can get within easy camera range before the bird spooks.

On ski tours near Cascade Pass we've had ptarmigan come right up to our tent and wake us before dawn with their clucking, which sounds as if they somehow disapprove of us. When the sun rises they disappear. While skiing to Camp Muir we saw a ptarmigan walking toward us. It kept on coming and finally walked right over Bob's skis and continued on, clucking constantly, never so much as looking at us. I didn't think *our* camouflage was that good.

MOUNTAIN BIRDS

Fall, when berries are ripe, is the best season for birdwatching in the mountains. We then see the beautiful bluebirds along with Steller's jays and even robins, which I somehow always associate with gardens and lawns at sealevel.

In summer a great joy when walking valley trails is hearing the little song sparrow bursting forth in arias. It's worth stopping a minute to find and watch this small nondescript bird with the beautiful voice. The hermit thrush is another songbird we sometimes hear but seldom see; my father-in-law is convinced that with its call it is saying, "Geranium, geranium, sweet William."

The mountain bird I'm fondest of is the camp-robber, a name given to both the Clark's nutcracker and the Canada jay. They look much the same but the nutcracker is larger, has white mixed with gray and black, and has a long beak. Both are noisy. Both live in the mountains summer and winter and descend on hikers and skiers at lunchtime to make off with crumbs or, if you're not careful, your whole sandwich. According to stories they'll steal food from a frying pan over a fire. I don't carry a frying pan so I can't vouch for that but I've had them land on a cooking pot boiling on my primus stove.

Camprobbers are a great source of entertainment at Paradise Inn. They watch from a tree and when they spot a chance for food swoop down, snatch what they can, and escape. Many tourists spend more time feeding the birds and ever-present squirrels than looking at Mt. Rainier.

I'd always wanted a picture of a chickadee, and one winter at Yellowstone they were all around the Old Faithful Visitor Center. I tried my telephoto but couldn't focus close enough. Then I put cracker crumbs on a limb and took pictures with my regular lens, holding the camera just 6 inches from the bird.

Hummingbirds buzz by in midsummer, often coming eyeball to eyeball with a hiker while investigating a red hat or red bandana. Once, while helping the Mountain Rescue Council pluck a hiker with a broken leg off Rampart Ridge in the Cascades, we lowered the stretcher right past a hummingbird's nest on a limb close to the ground. The operation stopped while rescuers and rescued all admired the tiny nest with one tiny egg.

A fascinating bird of wild areas is the dipper, or water ouzel, which continually bobs up and down as it scrambles along the shore of a lake or stream. In search of food it even walks under water. A ranger showed me a nest in a deep canyon just a few feet above the roaring Stehekin River in the North Cascades National Park. The nest was full of little ones and every time a parent came with food they let out a cry that could be heard above the river's roar.

Baby grouse with almost perfect camouflage, High Divide, Olympic National Park

101

Mountain chickadee at Old Faithful

Clark's nutcracker, Crater Lake National Park

BALD EAGLE AND SNOWY OWL

In the lower 48 states the bald eagle is an endangered species, the U.S. Fish and Wildlife Service estimating there are only about 1000 nesting pairs. Some ranchers with airplanes consider it sport to gun down eagles from the air. It's suspected others are shot for the tail feathers, in demand for imitation Indian headdress. Loss of habitat, though, is the biggest problem.

The greatest eagle show left in the lower 48 must be along the Skagit River near Marblemount, near the edge of the North Cascades National Park. In December and January between 80 and 100 eagles gather on a 3-mile stretch of the stream to eat spawned-out salmon. I've seen 50 or 60 at a time but haven't got many good pictures because it rains most of December and January. Also, though they're used to cars and boats, they fly off if a person detaches himself from a car. How long the show will continue is a question—the eagle site on the Skagit is being considered for a vacation-home subdivision and if that happens, as far as eagles are concerned there goes the neighborhood.

Hiking the Olympic Park Ocean Strip we frequently see bald eagles perched on sea stacks or snags. With a 5-foot wingspread, it's magnificent when flying but equally majestic sitting straight and tall atop a snag, the white head and tail of the mature bird making the statue perfect. Immature birds are a spotted brown, not developing adult markings until about 5 to 6 years old.

The San Juan Islands have a small year-around population, a dozen or more living on San Juan Island itself. The last 3 years a friend of ours there has boasted a pair nesting in his back yard, raising one eaglet a year. I spent an afternoon watching them on the nest, occasionally glimpsing a bit of fuzz—the eaglet. The birds are accustomed to our friend but were a bit upset with me.

Another large bird I always find exciting is the owl. Due to their nocturnal habits we rarely see them, but often enjoy listening to the spooky hootings in the night.

The species I'm most familiar with doesn't even belong in Puget Sound country. And the reason we see it so easily is it's not nocturnal, coming from a land where summer days are light for 24 hours. The snowy owl lives on the Arctic

Bald eagle on San Juan Island, Washington

tundra, feeding mainly on lemmings. Every few years something happens and great numbers head south. They've been observed in Redwood National Park and I photographed one at Tule Lake in California. Why the strange move south? Apparently it's an example of nature's balance-keeping system but the mechanism isn't exactly clear. Presumably a shortage of lemmings, however caused, triggers the migration.

Not being migratory by instinct, the snowy owl doesn't know how to return north. Those we see in the lower 48 are wandering aimlessly in an alien environment, unable to go home, and aren't long for this world. Knowing this makes me not so happy as I otherwise would be when watching the beautiful large bird, almost pure white, beak hidden by feathers, giving the impression of two large eyes without a face. The owl is impressive enough sitting but sensational flying, the long, narrow wings cleaving the wind.

The winter of 1973-74 was the Year of the Snowy Owl on Puget Sound. I heard that 30-40 had descended on the Skagit Flats and called the game preserve to find out if it was true. The officer said they'd had 6 but hunters had already killed them. (Though protected by law, the great birds are irresistible targets to certain "sportsmen.")

Pat and I went searching the back roads of the flats anyway, spotted one on a barn, and stopped for a picture. As I was focusing I happened to look up. On a telephone pole directly above were two more owls supervising my work. When I shifted my attention to them one flew off but I exposed two rolls of film on the other. He was still supervising when I finally turned the camera back to the barn-top owl.

Overleaf: Bald eagles on San Juan Island and snowy owl near small town of Edison on the Skagit Flats, Washington

Bald eagle on nest, San Juan Island

OSPREY

The plaintive cry of the osprey is unforgettable. The bird makes other noises, too, but the cry is a special distress signal that rends your heart.

Rangers at Grand Coulee National Recreation Area steered me to a nesting area on the Sanpoile River. I found a nest on a snag and saw one bird. It immediately flew off, circling a few feet over my head, then higher and higher until merely a tiny speck in the clouds.

Atop another snag I spotted a second nest with three osprey. I know my afternoon-long presence bothered them because they kept giving that plaintive cry. However, they continued flying in and out. I was semi-concealed under the trees so whenever a bird returned it made a treetop-level glide over my hideaway to see if I was still there, then spiralled several times and finally swooped to the nest.

I saw the three birds in the air together but never more than two on the nest at the same time. I can't figure how the third bird fit into the family scheme.

The afternoon was enlivened by a running battle with a crow. The crow was pestering the daylights out of an osprey, getting above and behind and diving into its back. What the crow thought he was accomplishing I've no idea, but it sure seemed a dangerous game.

The osprey being a fisher, the best bet is to look for them along streams. The first I ever saw was on the Yellowstone River. I'd just gotten back in the car after a session of photographing flowers when I spotted it hovering a hundred feet above the water. I grabbed my camera and leaned out the window. Two things happened at the same moment: The bird dived to the water and grabbed a fish. The car door flew open and I went sprawling on the ground. No picture.

Man has taken a terrible toll of the osprey. DDT accumulates in the adult's body, making the eggs so thin-shelled they can't be hatched. And in places like Yellowstone National Park it's in trouble because it must compete for food with thousands of human fishermen, and more every year. The old story—man does these little things he thinks are innocent, don't hurt anybody, and later discovers he's ruining the neighborhood.

Osprey watching nest

Overleaf: Sunrise on Crater Lake, Crater Lake National Park, a soaring area for hawks and eagles

Osprey and nest near the Sanpoile River, Coulee Dam National Recreation Area, Washington